Stars at Elbow and Foot

Selected Poems

1979 - 2009

Roger Moore

Island View
New Brunswick

ISBN: 978-81-8253-718-7

First Edition: 2021
Rs. 200/-

Cyberwit.net
HIG 45 Kaushambi Kunj, Kalindipuram
Allahabad - 211011 (U.P.) India
http://www.cyberwit.net
Tel: +(91) 9415091004
E-mail: info@cyberwit.net

Printed at Repro India Limited.

ACKNOWLEDGEMENTS

Early versions of some of these poems have appeared in the following magazines:

The Antigonish Review, The Aquinian, Arc, Ariel, The Canadian Literary Review, Casa de las Américas, Colibri, CommuterLit.com, Cormorant, Cross Canada Writers Quarterly, ellipse, The Fiddlehead, Nashwaak Review, Nonesuch Magazine, North York Arts Council Newsletter, North York Mirror, Poetry Canada Review, Poetry Halifax Dartmouth, Pottersfield Portfolio, Poetry Toronto, Quarry, Revelations, Waves, Wild East

I would like to acknowledge the help and encouragement I have received from my earlier editors, Fred Cogswell (Fiddlehead Poetry Books), Peter Thomas (Goose Lane), Denise Nevo (Mount St. Vincent University), and Stuart Donovan (Nashwaak Editions). I would also like to thank Dr. Karunesh Kumar Agarwal (Managing Editor, Cyberwit.net) for his help in publishing this book.

Allison Calvern, former host and organizer of Odd Sundays, earns my gratitude and a tip of my hat, "*Chapeau!*", not only for being my Beta reader for this selection and helping me choose, order, and revise these poems, but also for her friendship and her long- term dedication to, and enthusiasm for, poetry and creative writing.

Cover painting: ***Blue, blue day*** by Moo.

Introduction

Poetry has played a large part in my life. I read poetry, research poetry, introduce poetry to others, and also write it. Alas, I know more about French, Latin American, and Spanish poetry than I do about poetry written in English. Although I have taken multiple writing workshops, I have never taken a formal course on English poetry.

In 1962, while still at school, I received first prize for poetry at the Stroud International Festival of Religion and the Arts. This confirmed me in my determination to be a poet and, in 1979, Fred Cogswell published my first poetry book *Last Year in Paradise* (Fiddlehead Poetry Books). Then in 1986, Peter Thomas published my second, *Broken Ghosts* (Goose Lane).

From 1990 to 1993 mainly in conjunction with the Writes of Spring, which I organized as the Atlantic Provinces representative for the League of Canadian Poets, I printed and circulated six poetry chapbooks: *Idlewood*, *Secret Gardens*, *In the Art Gallery*, *Daffodils*, *Iberian Interludes*, and *On Being Welsh*. *Still Lives* (1989) and *Alban Angels* (1994), two unpublished manuscripts that reflect the deaths of my parents and their aftermath, received the Alfred G. Bailey Award from the Writers Federation of New Brunswick.

I visited Oaxaca, Mexico as a member of UNB's Oaxaca Exchange Program from 1995 to 2001. Here I developed an interest in visual art. My Certificate of Multimedia Studies (University of New Brunswick, 1999) dates from this period. My web page soon contained poems and photo poems based on Oaxaca. *Sun and Moon* (2000), *At the Edge of Obsidian* (2005), *Obsidian 22* (2007), and multimedia sequences like *Sun and Moon* and *Obsidian Prose Poems* were also inspired by these visits.

Denise Nevo (Mount Saint Vincent University) kindly edited these Oaxacan poetry books for me and along with them she published two more collections *Though Lovers Be Lost* (2000), and *Fundy Lines* (2002). Prior to my retirement from university teaching (2009), I printed and circulated three more poetry chapbooks: *Granite Ship — Poems from Ávila* (2006), *The Empress of Ireland* (2008), and *All About Angels* (2009). Finally, Stu Donovan, editor of the *Nashwaak Review*, published *Land of Rocks and Saints* (Nashwaak Editions, 2008). Selections from all of the above books are contained in the present collection.

A Poetics of Sorts

Approaching *The Empress of Ireland*

I first overheard those voices in the cries of the sea birds on the beach at Ste. Luce. Borne on the wind, over the sigh of the waves, they seemed high-pitched, like the voices of children, or of men and women in distress. These were lost voices, the cries of people alone and frightened by the dark. I heard them calling to me.

That night, little fists knocked at my cabin door and fingernails scratched at my window. Sounds, almost beyond the range of human hearing, imitated the snuffling of puppies when they turn over in their sleep and tug at each other, whimpering in their dreams.

"Who's there?"

I started from my sleep. But there was only the wind and the waves as the tide's footsteps climbed a moonbeam path to ascend the beach. When I walked on the sand next day, at low tide, I heard behind my back, the whispering of little voices crying to be set free.

"Who's there?"

A lone gull flew past my head and battered itself against the wind's cage with outraged sturdy wings. That night, the mist descended. The church stepped in and out of its darkness and shadows gathered, persistent, at my door. I walked out into the night and saw a lone heron surrounded by gulls. It was as if an adult, surrounded by clamoring infants, was standing guard over the beach. Then I saw the shadows of little children searching for their parents and the shapes of mothers and fathers looking for their offspring. Everywhere, feet shuffling through the tidemark, lonely people wandered among the seaweed and the sand.

Beyond them, on the headland, the church stood tall above the shadows. I saw family survivors, their lips moving in supplication, kneeling before the granite cross that stands above the sea. As I approached, they turned to me, opened their mouths, mouthed silent words, then disappeared. When I went back to bed, faces and voices visited me in my dreams. When I got up next morning, they came to me in the speech of birds hidden in the foliage, in the words dropped by the osprey's wing, in the click of the crab's claw as he dug himself deeper into the sand.

"Release us! Speak for us! Set us free!"

The words of The *Empress of Ireland* are not my words. They could never be my words. Foundered words, they are, flotsam and jetsam that I rescued from the beach, and dragged from the high tide mark filled with its sea weed, carapace, charred wood, old rusted iron, and the bright bones of long dead creatures polished by the relentless action of the wind, and the sandpaper sea.

Oaxaca and *Obsidian 22*

I cannot bring you the sounds and smells of Oaxaca. The pungent odour of the first drops of rain falling into dry dust, the tang of waxen candles burning in the cathedral's dark, the high notes sung at the golden altar in Santo Domingo by the old woman, dressed in black. Such things are beyond my talent to recreate, as are the bustling scents of the *abastos*, the bickering of rooftop goats, and the barking and growling of the dogs who patrol the *azoteas* at night while *castillos* burn, flames flow like perfumed water down church walls, and fireworks claw upwards into the sky to wake the sleeping gods with their noise and sparkle.

I cannot draw that knife edge slicing sun from shadow, heat from cool, that becomes in the verbal creativity of Octavio Paz, *solombra*, with its combination of sun and shade / *sol y sombra*, all in one neologism. Other things escape me: the taste and smell of sweat beneath the heaviness of the midday sun as it falls vertical from the sky and rebounds in waves from concrete and tar. Touch fails me too: the roughness of hand-hewn stone, the hardness of cobbles beneath the feet, the smoothness of silk contrasting with the harshness of tares in hand-woven wool.

We live in harsh world where poetry struggles to survive, where the great literary myths have been all but lost. Mass media rules. It sensationalizes and falsifies Here the power and glory of words is used not to delight and educate, but to manipulate the mind. We live, in other words, in the treacherous world of Descartes's evil genius, for we are constantly being misled. The Age, not of Enlightenment, but of Endarkenment, perhaps.

This is not the world in which I want to live. My chosen world is the quiet corner of the street where the leaves dance to the wind's tune. It is a world of mystery and dream, personal perhaps, but observable by any who have the eyes to see and the heart to sit still and listen. Is the world I create real? No, of course it isn't. It exists only in my head and on the page. Perhaps one day, if you travel to Oaxaca, you will see the things I have seen, and remember the thoughts I have thought, the words I have written, the world I have attempted to describe. But my world is as unreal as the words from which it is woven. This is the ***Catch 22*** faced by all poets.

Tolle, lege, vade mecum: take, read and come with me. Our journey will be a verbal journey into the heart and soul of a fabric that is woven from chance words, accidental encounters, surprising dreams, and visions of a vanished time and place. Vanished, because, as Heraclitus once wrote: "We can never bathe in the same river twice."

Meanwhile, c*arpe diem*: seize the day. Hold it in your hands and treasure it while you may.

Contents

Three Poems from *Last Year in Paradise* (1979)

St. Mary Redcliffe

Time and Temple Meads
have begrimed your wand-thin spire,
the tallest in England.

You waved goodbye
to the Cabot boys,
Nova Scotia bound,
as they set sail.

Starlings lime your belfry,
gift and inspiration
of Merchant Adventurers,
that gentlemen's company.

Worms wriggle and gnaw
at your ship's figure-head,
harbored now, bare-breasted,
sturdy in your oak-beam nave.

Rust rustles and creaks
at the Edney Gates,
wrought to last centuries
by Bristol ironmasters,
themselves apprenticed
to learn time's laws.

Mist

Mist and I lose my bearings:
men become trees become men
and the clammy damp
waves through my bones.

Hollow sound of my feet
where wraith-like white
pools in the street.

I whistle:
and the moon gleams bright
with a wolf's sharp teeth.

Backstreets in Santander

You go from the beaches turn away from the waters
and walk with your warder through this catholic prison,
through the streets of this city where innocents die
and the guilty confess to pitiless crimes
in hide-bound confessionals of dark white-washed churches
that strut in the streets and the heart-breaking alleys
with washing at windows and black widows waving
as you consciously wander through past sins and problems
forgetting, remembering the squares with their fountains,
with their saints and their statues in cold heartless marble,
with swords without edges and tongues sharp as grass
that cuts you with silence as it slips through your fingers
whilst bitter and bleeding you wander through labyrinths
of meaningless shortcuts leading to churches
and stationary statues that threaten with footsteps
until you come out at last to the light and the sea.

Eight Poems from *Broken Ghosts* (1986)

Butterflies

We raise our hands: you sever them at the wrist.
We spread out our arms: you measure us for a cross.
Where do we turn? Our fingers bleed from scratching
our skulls in bewilderment. They catch on the thorns
you so thoughtfully provided. Stigmata? No, you haven't
nailed us yet. Great barbed hooks penetrate our
bellies, inflaming our guts. Like live bait, threaded to tempt
Leviathan, we squirm. Like butterflies prepared for your
chloroform jar, we tremble. Your collector's pin is poised:
we await the final thrust that will skewer our bodies
and frame us under protective glass forever.

Winter Retreat

Ahead, the pass twists sharply to the heights
where starlight sharpens the ice that will slice
their bootless feet. For tonight, the slit-bellied
warmth of this horse they sacrificed for heat.

Fresh snow settles on the soldiers' coats.

Backs to a wind that freezes perspiration,
they gather like patient cattle that wait
outside some slaughterhouse for the welcome
sight of the friend who carries the butcher's knife
and, with a *coup de grâce*, ends their misery.

Catching, caging, and making them sing

We track them through their courting ceremonies,
hunt them down by the noise they make,
clutch them tight between anxious fingers.
We weave grass jails,
sentence them one by one to green imprisonment.
At day's end we ferry them to city apartments,
incarcerate them like canaries in their cages,
and wait for them to sing.
At first they are silent in this strange environment.
We feed them with bread dipped in brandy and wine.
Sooner or later they will sing in their captivity.
Now they will not eat.
They await the liquor that burns them
into fiery tongues of song.
Our midnights are haunted by their spirituals.

In the Sistine Chapel of Romanic Art San Isidoro, León, Spain

Pastoral scenes crowd the ceiling:
Annunciation, Nativity, and simple
shepherds kneeling. King Herod
orders all boy babies slain. Blood
drips from spears and swords as
children are spitted and split.

A rooster crows as Peter denies
his master, yet again. Pontius Pilate
calls Christ before him, on trial,
then turns and washes his hands.

Imprisoned in his Mandala, a smile
on his face, the Pantocrator holds
his fingers in an eternal blessing.
A million eyes have seen him there
and marveled at the universal love
contained in his oval expression.

Color, light, and boundless joy flow
down from the remaining paintings.

Eight feet up from the floor, art's
miracles cease. French soldiers stabled
their horses here. Cavalry stuffed carved
fonts with fodder to feed their mounts.
Illuminated manuscripts started their
cooking fires. Rood screens, hewn altar
rails fed the blazes' fury. They turned
chasubles, crosses, and candlesticks
into silver bricks, while the horses
snorted, stamped their feet in fear,
and erased all artwork from the walls.

Lessons

"The earth is geoidal, i.e. earth-shaped."
These words, dictated to me when I was
fifteen, taught me that teachers didn't
know everything there was to know.

Nor did they need to be know-it-alls.
"I don't know. I'll have to check," breaks
the great chain of the infallibility myth
but establishes links of understanding.

"What do groundhogs eat?"
"Spaghetti," says the grade two teacher
to my eight year old daughter who has
watched the groundhog devour
New Brunswick violets in our garden,
"with mushroom sauce, of course."

Lorca

Solidarity screamed out from posters
and stamps that carried snapshots of the dead
poet's face. We still haven't found his body.

He said we never would. They tortured him first,
taunted him for being homosexual,
trussed him up; laid him face down; then shot him,
for a joke, in the offending area.

He took a long time to die. When he did,
his body was dumped in some way out
ossuary. But first they carved the bullets
out of his corpse, three from the anal tract,
keeping them as souvenirs.

Next day his followers were put to death.
Waverers were soon convinced by bullets
lodged at the base of another's skull.

Later that week, Fascists, drunk, laughed uproariously
in their favorite bars. They dropped the bullets
into white wine, watched the blood trail as they sank,
and drank to the re-establishment of law and order.

This carving may be gently touched

It doesn't act like a bear. It has a Cocker
Spaniel's stop. Its jaws are wedged in a
grin. Its tongue hangs still. No saliva drops
from its chin. Motionless eyes. This carving's
tame. Children sit safely on its back, may stroke
the mighty muscles. It's safe. Woodworm,
like moth, have left holes in its back. More:
many a crack ensures its tameness. Its shoulders
hunch. Sixteen claws probe at the concrete museum
floor. Its nearer ear is chipped like my grandmother's
tea-set. There's lots of room for slips between cups
and this bear's lips. Yet I can sense death's closeness.

Suddenly, I know you're in there, Bear, alive, alert,
angry, hungry. When I feel you move beneath me:
cold sweat covers my false, carved skin.

The Naples Manuscript

I came to see the Naples Manuscript.
Its corrections are autograph, penned
by the poet himself. Ripped and torn,
blackened and scarred by acidic ink,
light leaks through it when held up.

Today I cannot see the volcano. Mist
covers the bay and the sun's been lost.
Warships in the harbor bob at anchor.
American sailors set free for shore
leave flood through the cafes and bars.

In dressing gown and nothing else
I work at the table in my room.
My face in the mirror wears a frown.
What did I come here to find? Light
slants upwards through shutter slats.
A tiny flaw walks shadow men upside
down across the ceiling. Graceful
as they are, they cannot replace
your face. In Madrid, we did as we
pleased. We lived together, travelled
together, had such wonderful times
in libraries, parks, museums, and bars.

Now I cry myself to sleep. How long
can we afford to be apart? One whole
week now. Phone calls to you break
my heart. Do you still love me?

Six Poems from *Idlewood* (1990)

Autumn

Pebbles have caught in my throat.
The word-river once flowing smooth
now backs up to spill leaf-freckled foam
over the tiniest barriers of branch and weed.

When I speak, some gypsy I find
has stolen my tongue, and my voice
is that of a changeling whisked away
from the cradle whilst her guardians slept.

Now leaves outside my window grow
rusty with autumn rain. A sharp-shinned hawk
no bigger than the blue jay he stalks
drives like a whirlwind at our feeder.

In dawn's early light, a Great Barred owl
flaps enormous wings and drops like a stone
on my favorite cat, lifting her up and away.

Old Eight Hoots

Winter has touched us with this change of clocks
and darkness clutches now an hour or so too soon.

Old eight hoots waits in the tree; he calls: I cough;
but he will not swoop down. He sits tight-perched,
out of sight, and chills me with his ghostly chorus,
hoo-hooing me home. Bright stars crackle the sky.

Frost crisps leaves. A mist weaves webs scarce-seen.
All around, as the cold ground creaks its wordless
tongue-tied whispers, night shapes abound.

Blue Jays at the Feeder

All the city alive in bed
waking to greet the bells
this Sunday morning
up you slug-a-beds
church bells call

The bells in this wilderness
are blue jays cracking
morning's silence
with shrill breakfast cries
from the garden feeder
weighed-down outside my window
by jumbled tumbling jays

It rocks with their weight
while starlings cast a blanket
black with gleaming seams
across a lawn glossy beneath
low-angled late fall sun beams
high-lighting speckled ice
as bright as imperial diadems

Oh bright knell of beauty
soon to be brought to ground
this frost-crossed winter

Wild Bird

Some wild bird has nested in my heart
and its blood-beat flutters new rhythms
as birdsong streams sunlight in my pulse

Afloat I knew the sea-surge lift and pull
now hot blood swells with the sun and sets
with this glorious fall from sky to earth
sweet helter-skelter glide of currents and blood

Hair is to head as feather is to nest
my egg-shell skull shows fine hair-line cracks
from the pecking of fine-tuned baby beaks

Cactus in Winter

Time delicate as an old man's beard
wraps itself around the cactus on the shelf
my tears are woven into empty dreams

Memory's many-colored cloak warms me
in this northern winter's pitiless chill

Oh pity this poor red tulip suffering now
as St. Valentine's Day drifts into history

It bends to touch the toes of its own mortality
while brother daffodil shrivels and turns brown

Outside my window a sky like a five-barred gate
where flocks of woolly clouds bleat white silence

Why?

In the mud nest jammed tight against the garage roof,
tiny yellow beaks open and close, showing colored throats.

Parent birds sit on a vantage point of electric cable,
mouths open vomiting silent calls
to chicks that demand a different response.

A sudden rush, a clamor of wing and claw,
a small body thudding down a staircase of air
to crash beak first onto the concrete floor.

"Why?"

"Wye is a river.
It flows through Ross-on-Wye
and marks the boundary
between England and Wales."

The swallows perch on the rafters
watching their fledgling
as it struggles on the floor:
weakening wing flaps,
last slow kicks of twitching legs.

"Why?"

"Y is a crooked letter
invented in days gone by
by the Green Man of Wye."

Four Poems from *Secret Gardens* (1991)

Swans Swimming

You swim so much better than I; one length,
two and your grace in the pool: stiff-necked,
swanlike. I think of white feathers, fine throats,
dark feet paddling beneath clear water.

Swans follow the ferry across the River Stour.
Yellow bills, sharp against the boat, crave the crusts
the ferryman keeps in a bag by the engine.
When he smiles at you, my stomach tightens.
When he nods, you break bread and offer it to the swans.
Round black buttons of eyes judge distance to perfection.
Can these sleek wings really break an arm or a leg?
Serrated edges on wicked bills
make short work of stale bread, iron hard.

Chlorine stings our eyes. Swimming side by side,
lids tightly closed, we dream our way across the pool:
ten lengths, then twenty. Later: your body above me,
partners in an ancient aquatic balle, *Leda and the Swan*
performed to perfection.

Wheelbarrow Poem

Once, an inmate at Cefn Coad, the Swansea
lunatic asylum, walked around the garden
with his wheelbarrow upside down
so nobody could put anything in it.
Not so crazy, eh? And that's what you and I
are like, without each other: upside down
wheelbarrows, or wheelbarrows with the floor
boards missing and everything falling out.
So here's my Valentine's Day card for you.
I've drawn an upside down wheelbarrow,
missing a wheel, and a watering can with a hole.
Look as hard as you like, there's not a flower
in sight. Anyone can give or get hearts and flowers.
Only someone really special merits a wheel-
barrow, missing a wheel, and upside down,
with everything fallen out.

Goodrich Castle

I thought I had felt everything worth feeling
until I visited Goodrich Castle and explored
with you its walls and towers and labyrinth
of inter-connected corridors and rooms.

Do you recall the way its old stone bones
thrust out from that pelvis of red bedrock?
Civil War tore down its curtain walls,
fired its stables, drove horses and people mad

with fear. Sometimes at night fate mans the pumps
of my blood and sends fire alarms surging through
my arteries and veins. No, I don't want to die

before you. I don't want to leave you here
alone, defenseless, besieged by memories
that gnaw at you, devouring your days, like flames.

Monet at Giverny

on receiving the book as an anniversary present

Everybody needs a secret garden. At Giverny,
Monet finally found peace. Look at these photos:
he walks between irises and nasturtiums on a gravel
path that leads to the Japanese footbridge that spans
his water lily-pond. Now he stands on the bridge.
Below him, clear in the water's mirror, eyes, mouth,
whiskers, hat, all drift, half-submerged, drowned
forever in the fragrant colors he turned into flowers.

Blank ghosts of his smile haunt the lily-pond's depths.
They mouth strange secrets that float upwards through
these colored prints. And now, in our new house, this
Christmas Eve, with snow on the ground and a chill wind
blowing a Queen Anne's Lace of drifting flakes against
the fly-screens, anniversary flowers brighten our table
while under the tree, the presents are piled and everything
waits, breathless, as past present, and future, hand in hand,
dance to the rhythm of the log fire's flickering flames.

Three Poems from *In the Art Gallery* (1991)

Portraits by Velásquez

Velásquez sought asylum in Canada and set up
his studio on the shore at Glace Bay.
He photographed short, stunted people working
underground in Cape Breton mines.

He blew up their photos to NHL size,
waited while they shook or coughed,
had patience till they were still, then "Flash!"

Coal-seamed faces, slack jaws, crow's foot eyes,
"Man's greatest sin is having been born,"
some seem to sigh. Others seek themselves
through stormy seas of inner darkness.

They probe gloomy galleries with Davey Lamp eyes
but find no gold, just clinging dust that clots their lungs.
Salvation Army Second Hand clothes lay siege
to tortured flesh that almost never sees the sun.

"Life is a snap," the photographer cries.
"And every photograph a lie."

Family Portrait

(After Francisco de Goya)

"On the left, his mother's side,
all looking like her;
his grandmother:
a witch without a broomstick.

On the right, his father's side,
all looking like him,
vague, vacant creatures
smiling inanely at the painter
they paid to mock them.

In the middle, their little boy —
each side has taken him by an arm
and they're slowly tearing him apart
in an uncivil tug-of-war."

Saturn

(after Goya)

His white hair flairs out:
strands spun by an albino spider.

His new-born infants struggle at first:
luckless flies in a fatherly parlor.

His mouth scurries over their bodies
assessing their warmth and nourishment.

Head first, like jelly babies,
he devours his sons.

Eleven Poems from *Daffodils* (1992)

Daffodils
(for my mother)

Light in dark
bright yellow stridence
shrill golden dog's bark
to warn off death's wolves
that freeze her blood

she dreaded night's unease
the devil's wintry anti-spring
life's darkest sparks

but loved the daffodils'
sunny March cadence
of brief piercing dance

Fishbones

Out in the garden, onions push through a pride of trumpeting daffodils. It's easy to make mistakes: they were all just bulbs when my mother planted them. Forget-me-nots twine intricate patterns, a fantasy of reds, greens, blues, between runner beans. I pull them apart with clumsy fingers, yet they knot again each day like the overnight tangles I tackle in my daughter's hair.

I am teaching myself how to braid by plaiting loose strings. I can manage two bunches now, one on each side, but it's much more difficult to part it neatly into three and to attempt that one thick plait she loves down her back. As for fishbones and French braiding... She begs me to try. I promise that when my thumbs turn into fingers, I'll give it a go.

Last winter, a heavy snowfall toppled the garden wall. Bricks and mortar litter the grass in untidy piles. I take my girl child by an arm and a leg and swing her round, faster and faster till, dizzy, she can hardly stand. I let her go and she staggers like her grandfather, who stumps round the garden leaning on two canes and jabbing at the wall he wants me to rebuild. He claws, with twisted fingers, at words, like fishbones, braided in his throat.

Death and the Maiden

Death is the washing machine no longer working.
It's the hot water tap drip, drip, dripping for want of a washer,
one dog, unclipped, unclean, where last year there were two.
It's meals forgotten on the stove, burned, and thrown out cold;
false teeth grinning on the sideboard or left to drown in plastic
yogurt pots half-filled with filthy water. It's milk bottles left
on the front door-step with holes pecked in their tops by birds.

Upstairs, in bed, the maiden lies asleep. She waits for the nurse's
step or the doctor's call and dreams of something beyond her fingers.

Web

I think of you walking the house, upstairs,
downstairs, out to the garden, at first, a glass
in your hand and then a bottle. You struggle,
strangled half-poisoned in spider webs
woven from bottled sunshine, circling
empty rooms, trapped in a domestic
cul-de-sac, lost behind locked doors,
peering through cobwebbed windows
that reveal no exit

First World Ward

snipers with telescopic sights
would shoot at the sound of a voice
but not of a whistle

it was unlucky then to light three
cigarettes from the selfsame match
one for the sniper to sight
two to aim and three to fire
one of three friends
left wounded or dead

no one in the ward is allowed to smoke
matron talks of chest infections
but she knows it's unlucky when patients
gather in groups of three and four and
feed from the same lighted match

my father whistles for attention
through the gaps in his teeth

Rings

One day, she gave all her rings to my daughter.
Next day, she took them back. "Give and take,"
we thought, but didn't complete the proverb.

Later, as she sickened, she circled the house
all night and brooded about unknown people
breaking and entering, wanting to steal her rings.

One night, with my father fast asleep in bed, snoring
as usual, his good ear pressed deep into the pillow
so he wouldn't hear her constant chiding, she emptied
her jewel-case and hid everything, everywhere, all
over the house and buried in the garden she hid
thousands of pounds worth of family heirlooms.

One Christmas, my daughter asked to see her granny's jewels.
"They're hidden," came the whisper, "so robbers will never find them.
But I've forgotten where they are."

When she died, there was a treasure hunt round and round
house and garden like we'll never seen again.
"Finders, keepers; losers..." Well: we're all weepers:
every time a pin rattles through the vacuum cleaner
we empty the dust bag onto a paper, and with watery eyes,
we fall on our knees and search the dust pile for those rings.

Barnfather

"Barnfather might yet be the world's greatest artist.
He held an exhibition, once, in a Bristol gallery
and sold me his impressions of dark, ploughed fields,
golden hay stacked yellow in broken barns,
tumbledown buildings lit up by an orange sky.

For years it hung over my mother's fireplace.

After the funeral, each night, before going to bed,
I stare into the picture's depths. I can almost see
my mother sitting beside the open farmhouse window.

One day, soon, she will open the dark-beamed door
and walk towards me."

Snaps

I turn the house upside down in a desperate search
for photos of you. Letters, buttons, certificates of birth
marriage death tumble to the floor. When I finally find
some snaps of your wedding, I can hardly believe my eyes:
here are the bridesmaids and the groom and the best man;
there's your mother and father come to give you away …

but you have already gone. Dark bouquets of jagged blackness
hang in the space you used to inhabit. Someone has taken scissors
or a knife and had hacked you from your day of glory
leaving, with no sign of your body, an open, shadowy grave.

Last Day

Cardboard boxes stand stacked against the wall.
The basement is already empty.
We have no spare time.

We must clean and polish and make things shipshape.
The new owners will be soon here
claiming their keys and their rights of entry.

Empty bottles of old memories stand disordered:
quarrels, wild words, making friends again;
my mother's body slumped at the bottom of the stairs,
or lying senseless in front of the television;
her bloodless face pale above the stretcher
as they carry her away.

We launch a last desperate hunt through the empty house.
How much of our former lives can we capture?
How many memories must we leave behind
with that one last look through the closing door?

Letters

Each Sunday, in boarding school, after Chapel, a spider
crawled out of my ink-well then limped its octopus way
across my weekly letter. This was news, information
relayed back from the front, from the trenches where
the infant slogged away toe to toe with the enemy, never
knowing that he was the enemy when he went back home.

Class: such a small word with so many meanings. Working
class, sitting in class, top of it, bottom of it, out of it, once
in a while, for various reasons, including cash and accent,
or just the neighborhood, back street, industrial Wales.
"NOCD! NQOCMD! Not quite our class, my dear."

Today, Sunday, after breakfast, I sit here as I have done
for over forty years, and I look at the empty page I must
attempt to fill with a tidal flow of words. Why bother?
They're all gone now. There's no one left to write for anymore.

On Watch

The day I buried her,
I threw my watch into her grave.

Earth covered the coffin:
and my watch, a simple watch,
face like a flower,
ticked towards silence.

Post Script

When there was nobody
left to write to
I taught myself to write
for myself

I took lessons
in the dark crevasses
of my secret heart
each flame a flower
thrusting through roots
of dry bitter ash

Deeper and deeper
into the silent rock
till my heart split asunder
and created new galaxies
of starry-eyed lies

Five Poems from *Iberian Interludes* (1992)

In the Archaeological Museum
Granada

First showcase: jawbone, *homo sapiens*. Mirrors
show us its further side. Second showcase:
a Neanderthal forehead from a female, age six.
Then, it's broken pottery dug from a cave.

A reconstructed burial with sea-shell necklaces
holds two small sets of human bones as tiny
as a baby's fingers, ivories from a dislocated
piano that no longer plays. In another display,
spears, daggers, and a rusted sword guard the dead
warrior on his journey through the afterlife.

Cracks in man's knowledge run jig-saw fine lines
through earthenware crockery. Holes in beakers
are windows on the past with fossilized faces peering
through. How much do we really know? And what do
they mean, these suns, rays, moons, lines, stars
gouged deep by men destined to die, yet certain
to live forever in their glass-bound graves?

Capella dos Ossos

(Evora)

The bull's blood spills: red wine on yellow sand.
His body, a broken vessel that black-plumed horses
drag from the ring. The air reeks with perfume:
essence of bulls' and horses' guts cut into streamers
to adorn this gaudy holiday. We go from the bull
ring to the chapel and we retch at the stench:
bones form the ossuary's walls and ceiling. Looking
down, we see we are walking on the dead. We give
warm coins and the tour guide counts our heads
to make sure that nobody is missing and she has
all the entry fees. Around us black holes fill the empty
sockets that form caves in long-dead skulls. Beside us,
bony arms and hands stretch out to welcome us in.

Rainstorm

Granada

Black umbrellas burgeon beneath sudden rain.
Black cloth opens to provide protection.
Churches fill with defenseless passersby.

The cigarettes they smoke flare shooting
stars through finger bars of flesh and bone.
After the rain, gypsy women flower in the street.

Carnations carve wounds in their sleek, oiled hair.
They offer good luck charms and fortune telling.

"Federico! Federico," the gypsies cry out,
"tomorrow, the guards will take you from your cell.
They will drive you to the hills and shoot you dead."

"Tonight," Federico replies, "I'll paint the city red.
And tomorrow ..." "Tomorrow," the gypsies sigh,
"the Alhambra will run red with your blood."

Snow in Granada

Columbus leaves footprints,
dark wake to his imagined ships,
in the snow; the unusual snow,
the snow they have not seen for forty years,
the snow that settles on roof tops forming
dark ridges where the sun is able to melt it.

The Alhambra under snow is a wonderland.
Stiff, starched buildings stand out
against the mountain's mass.
Tourists click their cameras
not knowing they are part of a miracle
for it snowed then as it snows now
and Columbus walked these streets
like any tourist, short of breath, short of cash,
the seams of his boots letting in the cold, wet snow,
you know how it is in winter on Main Street,
Any Street, Any Town in Canada.

And then the miracle: he is leaving it all behind him
when a messenger from the Queen catches him up
and says "Go for it: the ships, the dreams, the world,
they're all yours now!" And Columbus falls on his back,
moves arms and legs, creating winged shapes,
dream angels sailing through the snow.

Weltanschauung

(Alfonso the Seventh's view of the world
from the castle gardens in Almería.)

Inside thick, medieval walls: flowerbeds,
their blooms held fast by clinging earth
yet jailers in their turn to butterflies
and bees that clamp with dull damp feet
upon their sweetness to become enslaved
forever, as guitar-strings sweep cool waters
on this dying sun and I, Alfonso, the Seventh
of my line, dream bright new worlds to conquer
while my shadow stretches out across the plain,
and I clasp dream treasures in the palm of my hand.

The lone dove of my loveless heart struggles in
its trap of barren bone. All I see I own, yet my heart
is a walnut, shriveled in its wrinkled shell.

Seven Poems from *On Being Welsh* (1993)

Welsh miners

To be Welsh on the coalfield
is to speak the language of steel and coal
with an accent that grates like anthracite:
no plum in the mouth for us, no polish,
just the spit and phlegm that cut through dust and grit,
pit-head elocution lessons hacked from the coalface.

We sing deep, rolling hymns
that surge from suffering and the eternal longing
for a light that never breaks underground
where we live out our lives and no owners roam.

Here gas and fall spell violent death
and the pit-prop's creak is a song-bird
singing, then suddenly silent in its cage
to warn us of danger. Now song and heart
are stopped in our throats as, high above ground,
dark crowds of mourners slowly gather.

To be Welsh on Sunday

To be Welsh on Sunday in a dry area of Wales
is to wish, for the only time in your life,
that you were English and civilized,
and that you had a car or a bike and could drive or pedal
to your heart's desire, the county next door, wet on Sundays,
where the pubs never shut and the bar is a paradise
of elbows in your ribs and the dark liquids flow,
not warm, not cold, just right, and family and friends
are there beside you shoulder to shoulder,
with the old ones sitting indoors by the fire in winter
or outdoors in summer, at a picnic table under the trees
or beneath an umbrella that says Seven Up and Pepsi
(though nobody drinks them) and the umbrella is a sunshade
on an evening like this when the sun is still high
and the children tumble on the grass playing
soccer and cricket and it's "Watch your beer, Da!"
as the gymnasts vault over the family dog till it hides
beneath the table and snores and twitches until
"Time, Gentlemen, please!" and the nightmare is upon us
as the old school bell, ship's bell, rings out its brass warning
and people leave the Travellers' Rest, the Ffynnon Wen,
The Woodville, The Antelope, The Butcher's, The White Rose,
The Con Club, the Plough and Harrow, The Flora, The Pant Mawr,
The Cow and Snuffers — God bless them all, I knew them in my prime.

Sheep

Wales is whales (with an *aitch*) to my daughter who has only been there once on holiday, very young, to see her grandparents, a grim old man and a wrinkled woman. They wrapped her in a shawl and hugged her till she cried herself to sleep suffocating in a straitjacket of warm Welsh wool. So how do I explain the sheep? They are everywhere, I say, on lawns and in gardens. I once knew a man whose prize tulips were eaten by a sheep, a single sheep who sneaked into the garden on market day when he left the gate ajar. They get everywhere, I say, *everywhere*. Why, I remember riding in a passenger train and seeing five sheep travelling on a coal truck leering, like tourists travelling God knows where and bleating fiercely as they went by. In Wales, I say, sheep are magic. When you travel to London on the train, just before you leave Wales at Severn Tunnel Junction, you must lean out of the carriage window and say "Good morning, Mister Sheep!" And if he looks up, your every wish will be granted. And look at that poster on the wall: a hillside of white on green, and every sheep as still as a stone, and each white stone a r*oche moutonnée*.

Swansea

To be Welsh in Swansea is to know each stop on the Mumbles Railway: Singleton, Blackpill, the Mayals, West Cross, Oystermouth, the Mumbles Pier! It's to remember that the single lines turn double by Green's ice-cream stall, down by the Recreation Ground, where the trams fall silent, like dinosaurs, and wait, without grunting, for one to pass the other. It's to read the family names on the War Memorial on the Prom; it's to visit Frank Brangwyn in the Patti Pavilion and the Brangwyn Hall; it's to talk to the old men playing bowls in Victoria Park. It's to know that starfish stretch like a mysterious constellation, at low tide, when the fishnets glow with gold and silver, and the banana boats bob in the bay, waiting to enter harbour, and the young boys dive from the concrete pipes without worrying about pollution. But when the tide turns, the Mumbles Railway has been sold to a Texan, the brown and yellow busses no longer run to Pyle Corner, Bishopston, Pennard, Rhossili; sweet names of sand and tide, where my father still fishes for salmon bass, casting his lines at the waves as they walk wet footprints up the beach to break down the sand-castle walls I built to last forever on the Swansea sands.

Gower

To be Welsh in Gower is to spell it funny and pronounce it worse: Gŵyr. It's to know how to say Pwll Ddu. It's meeting the cows in the lane to Brandy Cove and knowing them all by name and reputation, which one kicks, which one gores, when to walk in the middle of the lane, and when to jump for the safety of the hedge. It's to know the difference between the twin farmers Upper Jones and Lower Jones. It's to recognize their sheepdogs, Floss and Jess, and to call them with their different whistles. It's knowing the time of day by sun and shadow; it's knowing the tide is in or out by the salt smell in the air without ever needing to see the sea; and now, in this far off land, it's hearing your stomach growl for *crempog, caws wedi pobi,* or *teisen lap* whilst memory's fish-hook tugs at your heart like your father hauled at salmon bass in Rhossili, Pennard, and Three Cliffs.

On Being Welsh in a land ruled by the English

I am the all-seeing eyes at the tip of Worm's Head; I am the teeth of the rocks at Rhossili; I am the blackness in Pwll Ddu pool when the sea-swells suck the stranger in and out, sanding his bones. Song pulled taut from a dark Welsh lung, I am the memories of Silure and beast mingled in a Gower Cave; tamer of aurox, hunter of deer, caretaker of coracle, fisher of salmon on the Abertawe tide, I am the weaver of rhinoceros wool. I am the minority, persecuted for my faith, for my language, for my sex, for the coal-dark of my thoughts; I am the bard whose harp, strung like a bow, will sing your death with music of arrows from the wet Welsh woods; I am the barb that sticks in your throat from the dark worded ambush of my song.

In the Cave

(Brandy Cove, Gower)

No: I do not understand these things. I have had few visions; no bush has actually burned for me. Though I have sat in this cave for many a day there has been no thunder, no earthquake, and no thin, small voice has called my name. I have only heard the wind and the waves and the sigh of the seabirds endlessly flying. Who set the curlew's cry between my lips? Who dashed the salt taste from my tongue? I will never forget the wet sand foaming between my toes nor the cracked rock crumbling under my hand ... yet I never fell, nor was I trapped by the sea below.

Five Poems from the Unpublished Alfred G. Bailey Prizes for Poetry — *Still Lives* (1989) and *Alban Angels* (1994)

Army Worms

Our garden is their training ground. They meld
into slithering shapes that frighten predators.

They wear camouflage and hide in the foliage
before swinging into action. The wind twirls them
as they dangle from their silken threads.

Last week, there was an accident on the firing range:
a tank turned turtle and rolled upside down:
two men inside died before the rescue team arrived.
Soldiers' families are trained to expect the worst.

But can we be trained to accept the day
our son shot skyward through the windshield,
his first car skidding on a convoy of army worms
weaving a slippery carpet across the road?

Our daughter walks to school
down the middle of the street.
She refuses to saunter beneath the trees.

She hates those silk threads drifting,
winding a shadowy shroud to cover her face.

Bears

Think of pink salmon caught in pools,
plucked from water, tossed to air,
the catch stacked rainbow fired.

Winter now:
unsnubbable, lumbering overcoats
closeted, laid to rest;
seeking power in hibernation
till sun from summit melts frosty dark:
fresh heartbeats forged in forest's night.

Think alchemy:
prime matter moved safely in flask or jar.

Think circus stars:
the Great Bear leads the Lesser,
dancing to the trainer's whip,
tumbling from their pedestals.

Secure behind bars,
think fallen stars.

Frog Lake: the Opera

Frogs chant spring love songs from pond to ditch,
one note symphonies, croaks of joy that move
other frogs to ecstasy.

Boy frogs seek girl frogs, encouraging them to share
the splendors of ditch life, pond life,
in a pairing whose springtime union will employ
frog song to create still more singers.

There's joy in this calling, croaking, creating,
and where there's joy, there's laughter, love,
happiness, light, sun, brightness, flowing water:
everything frogs associate with spring.

Every night the frowning silence of frozen stars
wings deeper into memory.

Spring moonlight swings its cheerful love lamp.
Earth also sings.

Cave Painting – the Ceremony

"Bear grease," she said, "for strength,
hound hair for speed, wolf blood for tenacity."
The medicine woman anointed my body,
blessed my eyes, caressing them with
an eagle's feather. I went a week without food.
I licked water from the stalactites and stalagmites
and saw my eyes reflected in echoing pools.

My spirit soared away as I hunted the moon
through a curious heaven of blazing stars.
I aimed thought arrows and my backbone
arched like a bow as I envisioned the animal
that they would pierce and the tip-toe dance
of my beloved victims. Hunter and hunted
we circled back and forth in my dreams.

(
sun around moon around earth
around light around fire around
hunger around thirst around life
around death
)

Stillborn Brother

Mixing cell with self, he divided, multiplied,
grew and was grown in your watery world.

Suddenly, he was swimming,
thrusting, urgent, through your flesh
till his bones filled your belly and silent, blue,
he emerged to your bedroom's brightness.

A half-life hooked to an emergency machine,
he endured a while, faded, then finally failed.

After the flames devoured him, his untied
bones half-filled the miniature urn.

No burial in an earth he never knew.
You took him to high cliffs
and cast him to wind and sea.
He descended into the waves.

On the third day,
his shadow rose and took flight:
a dolphin over bright water.

Ten Poems from *Sun and Moon* (2000)

Inquisitor

He told me to read,
and plucked my left eye from its orbit.
He slashed the glowing globe of the other.
Knowledge leaked out, loose threads dangled.
He told me to speak and I squeezed dry dust
to spout a diet of Catechism and Confession.

He emptied my mind of poetry and history.
He destroyed the myths of my people.
He filled me with fantasies from a far-off land.
I live in a desert where people die of thirst,
yet he talked to me of a man who walked on water.

On all sides, as stubborn as stucco,
the prison walls listened and learned.
I counted the years with feeble scratches:
one, five, two, three.

For an hour each day the sun shone on my face,
for an hour at night the moon kept me company.
Broken worlds lay shattered inside me.
Dust gathered in my people's ancient dictionary.

My heart was like a spring sowing
withering in my chest
It longed for the witch doctor's magic,
for the healing slash of wind and rain.

The Inquisitor told me to write down our history:
I wrote … how his church … had come … to save us.

Monologue

"They broke our walls," Mono whispered, "stone by stone.
A new church they built on the land they stole from us.
Red was its roof from a thunderstorm of blood.
The white bones of their lightning scattered us like hail.

They ripped out our tongues and commanded us to sing.
Carved mouths were ours, stuffed with grass.
Stone music forced its way through our broken teeth.

Few live who can read the melodies of our silence.
We wait for some wise man to measure our dance steps.
Pisando huevos: we walk on tiptoe across
these stepping stones of time.

New Tomb at Huijazoo

Her favorite figures gazed down from the walls:
an owl, a jaguar, Cocijo, the Zapotec god of storms,
thunderous in red-and-buff funeral colors.
At her side, jade beads, gold butterflies, ceramic dogs.
Her family stayed for three short nights,
then they went away and left her in peace.

At first, she tried to count the days, but her mind
came unstuck around a hundred circles of the sun.
Between her and the world stood a thick wall of rubble.
Confused by the shadows, she lost count of the years.

A tall man arrived, blond, with a beard.
He ordered the people to break down the wall.
When they broke through, she awoke to harsh voices.
They took away her pottery, scattered her bones
in their search for hidden gold, and left her broken-
hearted, abandoned, and alone.

Opening the Tomb

The blond man spotted a known face in the crowd and cried
"To me, my friend! Come! Stand at my side!"
But the known face scowled, put on a mask, and showed its teeth.
Jaguar it became, or Death, and its flayed skin flapped.

"I have a document," the blond man said,
"from the Ministry of Science!"
He waved his papers in the air.
The people waved back: knives, clubs, machetes.
"Our ancestors are buried there," they cried.
"Leave them alone in dust and silence. Let them sleep!"

But the blond man ached for the bright gold buried in the tomb.
He turned away. The crowd rejoiced.
Next day he returned: with soldiers.

Then the fields were sown with bones and watered with blood.
New headstones sprouted overnight in the village.
Fresh mounds of earth, bright with flowers, white with crosses:
fresh treasures for more blond men to find.

Conversation Piece

The rich man in Yanhuitlan
bought a husband and wife
from a nearby village.
They cost nine *pesos de oro.*

Next day,
the high priest cut their throats
at the foot of a large stone statue
carved in the image of Tlaloc,
the god of rain and water.
Then he sprinkled the idol
with their blood.

"Now, he said, "the rains will return
and the crops will grow again.
The sun will continue his daily journey.
In blood we were born, my friends,
and in blood we will finish our days."

The sun's rising kiln fires the clouds with light.
Shadows shorten, grow fatter, and stronger.
The night ants (red) return to their nests;
the day ants (black) set out to plunder.

Wind of Change

"Softly, softly," she whispered,
"for at such times, earth's fires are low,
and if the wind blows wrong
and they go out,
then who is to replace them?"

She shuddered.
"For sheep and goats have eaten the grass
that bound the earth that held the trees,
and now there is no kindling.
"The magic sticks have gone from this world
and those foreign priests permit no sacrifice."

She paused then cried aloud:
"Put out the light!"

We sat together in the gathering darkness,
listening to the wind's footsteps
as it snorted and rooted at windows and doors.

The Scorpion

"Heal yourself," cried the *sânate* bird,
drawing his knife blade over sun-warmed stone.
Trees filled up with sparks of color.
Butterflies, yellow and black, spread delicate wings,
as they throbbed at the end of unseen strings.

Yesterday, in the rain, *Alacrân*, the Scorpion,
knocked at our door and asked to come in,
out of the rain. We told him to go away.
Tail in the air, he minced down the wet
garden path and faded out of sight.

Today, his carcass dries on a stone in the sun.
Black ants pick at his body.
They carry him in bite-size chunks back to their nest,
up the thin crack in the patio wall,
right past our now open door.

Santo Domingo

Worshipping Gaia before the great altar
in Santo Domingo

If the goddess is not carried in your heart
like a warm loaf in a paper bag beneath your shirt
you will never discover her hiding place

she does not sip ambrosia from these golden flowers
nor does she climb this vine to her heavenly throne
nor does she sit on this ceiling frowning down

in spite of the sunshine trapped in all this gold
the church is cold and overwhelming
tourists come with cameras not the people with their prayers

my only warmth and comfort
not in this god who bids the lily gilded
but in that quieter voice that speaks within me

and brings me light amidst all this darkness
and brings me poverty amidst all this wealth

The Dancer and the Dance

Skin drum, rattle of seeds in a sun-dried pod,
single violin string stretched across an armadillo's shell:
she binds me with a string of notes undone with her hair.
I am tense: an instrument waiting to be played.

The ghost of her melody tosses its head and plucks
stars to thread into daisy chains.
The full moon hangs its lantern in the sky.
My lover sculpts time and space into jewels.
She pins to my chest three small notes and a skeleton of words.

Scars layer my wrists and ankles:
star crossed bindings, cutting against the grain.
I gather a harvest of moonlight and she holds it in her eyes.
Nesting grasshoppers, her fingers in my hair.

When her lips touch mine
we know we will never be the same.
Together we weave a slender cage.
She cuts out my heart with her tongue
placing it on an altar inside the bars.
She locks the tiny door with a silver key
wrought from a moonstone.

My heart grows wings: when the cage door opens
they will fly me to her lips. Our last night together:
I pluck a blossom from the *tulipán* tree and place it
in the pocket of flesh where my heart once beat.

Tomorrow when the flower breaks,
it will stain my shirt with a damp splash of blood.
The scent of our happiness will endure forever.

Tangled Memory

night without moon without stars
dark sand dropping filling my mouth
I walk the lonely bed of a dried up river

when I stumble in my dream
my feet leave no footprints
colorless is my path
through shadow and sand

figures of darkness are conjured before me
hollow their eyes their mouths black caverns
no flesh decks their whitened bones

footless they sigh a sibilant song
mindless they draw in a net full of sorrows
silver fish darkling losing their sparkle

dusky shawl of a knitted dream
wrapped round my shoulders

I pick at knots of tangled memory
a word sharp as a stone cast at a friend
sea shells cutting naked feet at water's edge
sunlight weeping blood over mother-of-pearl

Eight Prose Poems from *Though Lovers Be Lost* (2000)

So Real It's Surreal

An elephant with a crane fly's spindly legs stands beside the bedside cabinet. Is the human body a chest of drawers to be opened and closed at will by other people, and things removed? On the operating table, a sewing machine and a bread knife wait inside a black umbrella for their next victim. Caught like a hedgehog in the glare of onrushing headlights and curled into a ball, are my words not more than wasted movements of throat, lips, tongue, and teeth? Limp kites with nothing to fill their paper sails, they hang on an old barbed wire fence lying tangled between us. The metallic star shell in the ceiling gashes harsh light across the no man's land where my mother now lives. The needles in her arm throw an ever-plunging sea of shadows. When I look at my watch: time flies off my wrist and flaps its hands.

Building on Sand

Everywhere the afternoon gropes steadily to night. Some people have built fires, others read by candlelight. Geese, drifts of snow their whiteness, settle on the riverbank. They walk on thin ice at civilization's edge. Around them, the universe's clock ticks slowly down. Who forced that scream through the needle's eye? Inverted, the Big Dipper, hangs its question mark from heaven's dark eyelid. Ghosts of departed constellations stalk the sky. Pale stars bob phosphorescent on the flood. The flesh that bonds, the bones that walk, the shoulders and waist on which I hang my clothes, now they stand alone and listen at the water's edge to the whispering trees. They have caught the words of snowflakes strung between the stars. Moonlight is a liquor running raw within them.

Lagartija

There are striations in my heart, so deep, a lizard could lie there, unseen, and wait for tomorrow's sun. Timeless, the worm at the apple's core, waiting for its world to end. *Seculae seculorum*: the centuries rushing headlong. Matins: wide-eyed this owl hooting in the face of day. Somewhere, I remember a table spread for two. Breakfast. An open door. "Where are you going, dear?" Something bright has fled the world. The sun unfurls shadows. The blood whirls stars around the body. "It has gone," she said, "the magic. I no longer tremble at your touch." The silver birch wades at dawn's bright edge. Somewhere, tight lips, a blaze of anger, a challenge spat in the wind's taut face. High-pitched the rabbit's grief in its silver snare. The midnight moon deep in a trance. If only I could kick away this death's head, this sow's bladder, this full moon drifting high in a cloudless sky.

Shadows and Sand

After heavy rain the house shrinks. Its mandibles close. A crocodile peace descends from the jaws of heaven. I no longer fit my skin. Iguana spots itch. Walls encircle me, hemming me in. When I lose it, whatever it is, my fingers pick at seams, hankies, skirts, shirts, jeans, or strip a label from a bottle; or they break bread, or there are so many things I do, personal things. On the table, a vacant cereal bowl, a silver teaspoon in a saucer, an empty teacup returning my round moon stare. My hands terminate in pointless needles. They unravel patterns then try to knit them together again. I toss three coins and the *I Ching* sloughs my fortune: each lottery ticket, a bullet, none with my number. Late last night I thought I had grasped the mystery: but when I awoke I clasped only shadows and sand.

The Painter and the Pond

Clad in an abyss of lilies, imperial his reflection, he slides to sleep, merging into his imagined dream. His earthbound ribs form an arch, a vaulted cathedral: immaculate the blood space, as heavy as a stone at Stonehenge this altar spanning downwards through a liquid, tumbling sky. Green footprints, the lily pads; a halo, this drowned man's beard, liquescent, like the gods he dreamed walked dry over water. The executioner stripes evening across the sacrificed horizon. "In blood we were born, my friends, in earth will we rest; our flesh turned to bread, our imperial wine empurpling with day's death this troubled sea." Exotic this sudden movement, *Carassius auratus* flowering their ruby thoughts of gold fish in this long thin line of maple clouds. *Le roi soleil* threatens to blind us: *rey de oros* the sun glow braiding itself an aureate palette in a susurration of floating, left over leaves.

Monet

Clos Normand and the *Grande Allée* closed to him now; folded his flowers, their petals tight at his nightfall; dark their colours, mourning for his mornings of light, fled far from him now. The Lady of the Lake holds out her hand and hands him an apple: *l'offrande du coeur*. A scarlet heart of flame and world and word regenerate in tulips. Especially when the dying sun spreads molten fire over a crimson lake and the limpid sky brims over into low clouds trapping a slash of colour here, and there a tree, a fountain of gold. If the sun is an apple blushing on a setting branch, the money plant is the silver-white of moonlight between fine-tuned fingers. When it rattles its seeds, coins blunt the moon's sharp edge, and earth is eclipsed by nickels and dimes. The breeze bowls clean dry bones across the sky. Wind of change: that first fast bite too bitter to remember and timeless this tide, this ebb and flow, this great pond-serpent coiled around the foot of the tree, devouring its tale, dictating itself to death, forever.

House of Dreams

The clematis unfolds bruised purple on the porch. Thelonius Monk: beneath the black and white hammers of ivory keys, old wounds crack open. A flight of feathered notes: this dead heart sacrificed on the lawn. I wash fresh stains from my fingers with the garden hose. Somewhere, the whitethroat trills its guillotine of vertical notes. I flap my hands in the air: they float like butterflies, amputated in sunlight's net. I hold up shorn stumps of flowers for the night wind to heal as a chickadee chants an afterlife built of spring branches. Pressed between the pages of my dream: a lingering scent; the death of last year's delphiniums; the tall tree toppled in the yard; a crab apple flower; a shard of grass as brittle as a bitter tongue at winter's end.

Cage of Flame

Now you are a river flowing silver beneath the moon. High tide in the salt marsh: your body fills with shadow and light. I dip my hands in dappled water. Twin gulls, they float down stream, then perch on an ice-floe of half-remembered dreams. Eagle with a broken wing, why am I trapped in this cage of flame? When I turn my feathers to the sun, my back is striped with the black and white of a convict's bars. Awake, I lie anchored by what pale visions fluttering on the horizon? White moths wing their snow storm through the night. A feathered shadow ghosts fingers towards my face. Butterflies stutter against a shuttered window. A candle flickers in the darkness and maps in runes the ruins of my heart. Eye of the peacock, can you touch what I see when my eyelids close for the night? The black rock of the midnight sun rolled up the sky. Last night, the planet quivered beneath my body and I felt each footfall of a transient god. When will I be released from my daily bondage?

Ten Prose Poems from *Fundy Lines* (2002)

Old Loyalist Burial Ground, Fredericton

The signs can be easily missed: a half-covered entrance, a single handrail. Two hundred years ago, those who did not survive that terrible first winter were buried close at hand. Golden dandelions with royal ruffs cluster beside deep wheel ruts. Red-shouldered blackbirds flit from branch to branch. Grosbeaks swarm like bees in black and yellow flocks. The river still flows fresh and high and fiddleheads thrust their creaking way through untidy debris. Inside the burial ground, two leaning stones, their inscriptions blurred like yesterday's half-erased chalkboard, mock the well-mown lawn and latest monument. Mosquitoes whine and descend in squadrons. Leeches rise, draw blood and, gorged, subside. Late sunlight clots its spring song earthwards. Seeds thrust impatiently to leaf and flower: underground bustle of root and hustling worm.

Crazy Glue

Yesterday, I got lost in the mirror. I know how to swim, but I would have drowned, except the light was too shallow and my feet touched bottom when I let the wheels down. I swam on and in looking for a deserted island on which to build my idle sand castle dreams. Two people said they saw my reflection swimming like a goldfish in the silver of that secret space. They said I stared back out at them with circles of longing ringing my eyes; but I laughed when they said they had seen me, for when I shaved this morning, I just wasn't there. My razor dragged itself over an empty space and its sharpened blade scraped white music from the margin of a cd rom that spun on edge like dust rings round a vanished planet. There is a black hole where my passport photo used to thrive. Someone plucked me from the circle and cut me out in the dance last night. Now I'm looking for a scrapbook into which to stick myself with crazy glue that will never, never come undone.

The Shadow

The janitor said that the shadow had been seen lying down at midnight on the corridor floor. Someone dialed 911 and a police car came with a bucket and a mop to sweep this nonsense under the carpet. But the shadow wasn't there; it must have climbed to its feet and scuttled away like a vagabond crab clicking its pincers over dry moonlight on the sanded floor. It ran to an elevator and the janitor watched as the needle jerked to a stop at every floor. Now there is a fear of shadows in the washrooms. People stare at themselves in the mirror and see the devil looking at them with an offer of work for idle hands. He is horned and hoofed and harsh of breath as they clean their teeth and leave the cold tap running. When the water's turned off, long, thin fingers pluck the strings of their hearts and a quaint fibrillation fills the silence of this haunted house.

Blind Date

You couldn't see the holes the doctor drilled in my head when he thought he was a woodpecker. You were oblivious to the bland, black splinters sprouting from my fingers and my neck. Unseen, the ladderback drowsed its feathered siesta as peace descended to my mind's cluttered attic. When push came to new love, the bluebird couldn't find the old silver ring I borrowed from the curtains. How could you care about its failure to sparkle in the sun? When you ran your fingers through my hair, you cut yourself on a feather's edge and my shirt rose up in the air and flapped with sudden writing, as red as blossoming flowers. You sensed their crimson dampness, but couldn't see the petals turning skywards to a pallid moon. The clockwork mouse ran down the tower. The clock struck the chaos of a universe at sixes instead of sevens and we knew we two would never be one. Before you drove away, you told me to keep my pity for falling leaves, for sparrows in winter, and for the defenseless chickadees who quest at the feeder and leave in fear of the kitchen cat with her dogged stealth: a game of paws and pause, crisp and silent through the green hair of the grass.

View from the Morning After

My dog breaks loose and howls for an hour at the half time orange stationed by the slithering stars. An owl's wing slices the night in two and bats make merry round the chimney. My sister's skeleton dances on a silver chain of incense. When they auction her clothes, they roll fresh dice on a skintight drum of thunder. I awake to the tap-tap-tap of melting ice as it hammers headlights into my peccant skull with a papal mallet. Splinters of memory lie buried in my heart: a white horse carved on a limestone hill; the grassy eye of a green glass circle; an empty uniform, full of bullet holes, tramping swiftly away. Green worms crawl from the apple's core, stretch out their hands and beg for more. Late last night an unpaid bill nipped at the postman's heels and a ghost slipped her arm through my letterbox to unchain my mail. I stretch my hand out to the morning news but it slips like water through my premature fingers. When the grey mist men return to my parents' house, I pour them a glass of concrete and ask them where they have parked my father.

Orpheus

I try to picture your face, but it has grown legs and walked out of my mind. What pencil can draw it forth from the depths of this hell I have sketched for myself? I walk away, but turn again to look. You are fading, failing, slipping away downhill, backwards into the shadows. I turn my back on darkness. Ahead lies sunlight where other women sing and dance. Whose is that head, floating downstream, lips drawn back in a silent scream? There are blood red berries at the rowan's foot and the mountain women have covered themselves in dust and ashes. Wednesday: the berries' torn flesh is fingernail bright. Thursday: an angry robin stamps on the tousled lawn and its Maundy song is a shriek of violence, a finger-nail torn from the flesh. Friday: the snapdragon opened the frosted forge of its mouth crowning the sky with ice-hard shards of shafted fire. Saturday, on the back porch, in a halo of mud and straw, two blue robin's eggs stare back at me, as accusing as hunger in a baby's face. Sunday: I retune my heart and scribble another song.

Snowman

The dog has forged his footpath through the snow. Each visit melts my feet a little more, and turns them yellow. Body and bawdy soul, I am locked up tight in this strange white corpse. Moon's celestial lamplight sparkles crow's feet over my face. A long time ago, a rain shower stole my smile. I threw all my keys down a deep, dark well. Now no one can open my heart's secret door to let in the sun. Earth's satellite flaunts its cat's cradle lantern: a flash of stringy flesh glimpsed at a nightclub. I dream I can press my frozen face against some lighted window and turn into bone and blood. Who planted these flowers in my skull and tuned those light bulbs in my head? Who gave me this carrot for my nose? Sometimes, at night, I can smell crisp crocus flames as they huddle beneath the snow, licking upwards to this summer sky-in-waiting. Frost breaks open the earth's bleak, iron womb. Crystal fingers, their fine rings sparking, reach up to pluck this fire plug snap of moonlight falling from a cloudless sky.

Big Hand / Small Hand

It's late in my life, with the big hand stuck on the nine, at a quarter to something, and the small hand twitching its red-tipped needle of blood. Yesterday, the breakdown van called for my body and towed me to the doctor's. "Cough!" she said. "Say ninety-nine! Now cough again!" All the while, cold hands probed my unprotected body. Bottoms up? Thumbs down? It's hard to see that the wine glass stands a quarter full when seventy-five per cent of the wine has gone and my empty skull lies drained on the operating table. I examine the palpitating heart they have torn from my chest. Flesh of my flesh, it beats in my hand like an executioner's drum. I hear the tumbril drawing near. My colleagues sharpen their knitting needles. My lungs are twin balls of wool knotted tight in my chest.

Raven

When Raven flies through his trap door in the sky, a light bulb clicks off in my head and I fall into darkness. Is there some safety net before oblivion? Raven's claws scar crow's feet on a fingernail moon; his bleak black beak widens the hole in my head and the Easter egg of my skull shows thin blue cracks. Outside my window, the river moves backwards and forwards with the tide. Raven shrugs at cancerous creatures, promising nothing. He soars into clear skies in search of his private exit and extinguishes sun, moon, and stars, plunging our world into blackness. The light on the point picks out a heron, mobbed by a clacking ring of gulls. The sea mist wraps the real world tight in its cloak. Now sea and lighthouse, heron and gulls, are distant things of memory. Raven, shoulders hunched, stands like a stone, an anthracite block hacked out from the coal seam in my mind, hand carved from feathers and my forefathers' blood.

Crucified Crow, Old Logging Road, NB

Head twisted to one side he watched us enter the woods. His fingers were splayed like feathers. Wide spread wings, he was nailed there, poised for instant flight. For how many revolutions of the sun had he hung in that space watching the world wheel by? Strung between two trees, wind and weather breaking him down into this lump of solidified silence. When we cut his body down, it folded like a pack of cards, all jacks, all black, all value peeled away in fifty-two faceless moments. I opened a door in my head to let in sunlight. It filtered through high, leafless branches, until the late spring struck a broken chime. Raven coughed. His voice was a cracked bell, inviting slow fires to explode a mine in the mine-field of my mind.

Seven Poems from *At the Edge of Obsidian* (2005)

Breakfast

Yesterday, I sacrificed a chicken.
Unborn, it lay within its calcium cocoon, dormant,
a volcano sleeping beneath a blanket of thick snow.
Tap, tap, tap: the silver spoon bounced off the ovoid head.
Suddenly, the shell cracked and spurted orange blood.

Today, I tap with my spoon on the grapefruit's papal skull.
Silence. Death is the sole inhabitant of its honeycombed pith.

High in the church tower, a hammer blow falls on an echoing
anvil and the cracked bell lurches into motion.
Rooster crows his thick, rich cocoa *rico* as he stands
on a dung hill of blackened torsos and fire-roasted beans.

A squeezed orange racked by the inquisitor,
its once rich golden robe spent and exhausted,
now lies in shreds, wasted rags torn from a worn-out moon.

What pale lantern wastes its life as it sails across a tabloid sky?
Naturaleza muerta: the orange expiring on the table, its carcass
still sticky, its life-blood a sacrifice, its golden liquid
as fierce and as sweet as a butterfly perched on a sunlit branch.

Up and About

The sky is a sharp, blue guillotine
poised between buildings waiting
to sever the wings of butterflies.

Scorched circles of admirers:
anonymous holes in the crowd's
dark thunderstorm of faces.

Sun-polished *marimbas*:
a street musician stands in the shade
playing a bamboo *danse macabre*.

A heart of fire burns in an iron barrel.
The taxi's tumbril rattles down the street.
Who or what will be chosen next?

Last night the *castillo*'s towers
came tumbling down as a cataract
of flame flooded the cathedral's wall.

A black wooden bull danced with a tiger
in the main square, striking sparks from
horse hairy and licorice stripes.

A red spark burned my shirt, bored through
the cotton and sank tiger teeth into my skin.
Mescal makes me one with the grasshoppers.

I have forgotten how to walk in the woods.
I have forgotten how dead leaves tumble from trees.
Soon now, the *danzantes* will dance on my grave.

Balcony

A brightly feathered angel
sits a paradise's door.

Green, red, and yellow,
the parrot mocks his master,
burnishing the morning
by the light of the grapefruit's
glowing golden globe.

Poised on a sunbeam,
the hummingbird's soul
whirls sad worlds away.
Glistening pearls of dew
embellish morning's throat.

Red blood melts sealing wax
all over the hibiscus.
Bougainvillea strains purple stains
through a lonesome sift of sunlight.

The church tower shimmers,
insubstantial in this fragile air.
Leaning on the balustrade
I am suspended in space.

Mass in the Consolación

This is not a normal church. The lady in front of me opens
her blouse and offers her breast to her youngest child
who sucks greedily. The old man at the back holds a roll
your own smoke in the palm of his hand and closes his eyes
as he draws in the drug, holding it between tongue and teeth.
Three dogs, tongues lolling, have discovered the bitch in heat
who came here for sanctuary. They chase her up and down
the aisle as the high priest doggedly murmurs a blessing.
I have heard these words before; and all this music.
Bored acolytes pass the oil, and present the sacred wine.
Flowers flourish and candles flicker under the altar's crucifix.

Sacred words, secret worlds opening like oysters.
A laying on of hands. Footsteps going nowhere.
Seculae seculorum: hard, crisp sounds, white and sharp,
like the inside of an apple when strong teeth penetrate
the skin and saliva flows. Shadows reach out to caress
the unwary with the artificial incense of tranquility.
Yellow light marches across the walls. The church
warms up with song. Wide-open, staring eyes. That
young man nailed to his wooden frame, calls my name.
My live-wire mind turns into a pinball, rebounding from
pillars to paintings, trapped, unrepentant, in this circus.

Water

Cupped hands cannot embrace you. Do you remember when the earth
was without form and darkness lay on the face of the deep?
You yearned then to be released, to flow from darkness
and flower in sunlight. Images and symbols fly flags within my skull:
the shrunken head pond ringed like a bathtub, surrounding fields
scorched and dry. The land's parched throat longs for liquid:
water, born free, yet everywhere in chains. A mirage of palm trees,
standing against burning sand as the hot sun drags its blood red
tongue across the sky. Panting for water, I lick my lips like a great
big thirsty dog. Worlds begin with the "Let it be of light" as it divides
from darkness. Then comes the world, the inner waters in which male
and female forms are borne; when the waters break, the life sustaining
substance drains away throwing us from dark to light. The mid-day
sun hangs from the sky's belly like a ball-turret gunner, spraying
blood red wine over and under this double-barreled cloud of thunder.

Cortés's Sword

His old sword sits outside its scabbard
and howls like a dog that scents a full moon.

Its long tusk dwells on forgotten blood:
dead flesh carved over rock and dry stone.

Flintlocks and muskets have blunted the sword.
Bereft of sharpness, it hides in a coffin of rust.

Anonymous clocks wear Hallowe'en masks
to disguise the blankness of their faces.

After the earthquake, the museum's walls
longer hang perpendicular. A pendulum

dropped from the edge of the roof,
swings for a while, then settles heavily.

An opening door snaps a sudden match.
Tick of the death-watch beetle in
a crumbling colonial house.

Wingless in Gaza Street

amputees deprived of flight
they flutter grounded in the gutter

galley slaves chained to broken oars
they ply blunt stumps relentlessly

shorn of strength and beauty
their once glorious shuttles weave dark circles

my mouth is a full moon open in a round pink circle
bone and its marrow settle in subtle ice

futile fragility of the demented heart pumping
its frequency of fragmented messages

frail beauty torn from its element of air
this brightness of moths drowning in inky depths

the seven o'clock news brought to you
from an otherwise deserted street

Five Poems from *Granite Ship* (2005)

Heraclitus

Everywhere, taps of cold water, flowing,
water in which you can never wash your
own hands twice. Cold eyes stare back
from your morning mirror. This page of

life, as cold as a matinal razor blade,
turns slowly over. You know there are
agreements, deals you can never sign,
no matter how much you walk the line.

Words fall with the fullness of ripened
fruit: empty sentences, all meaning lost,
promises repeated, always to be broken.

This tap water, in which you can never
wash again, still flows. Untasted, untested,
untried the delicacies that lie before you.

Verracos

Moss grows slow and silent in the interstices
between thin grooves where this stone once
fretted and freckled itself. Chill at first touch,
it soon warms, then tingles beneath the hand
as fingers tighten infinitesimally. A life force
moves up from a focus lying centuries deep.
This stone's slow heartbeat, a pulse almost
too hidden to acknowledge, is still there, in
spite of the outside traffic's ceaseless tide.

Inside, a slower tide bears us on and in, deeper
into the hand-carved stone, the culture that cared,
their markers bared to the elements, all warriors
and worshipers long dead, their secrets locked
beneath earth, held down by stone, buried, long-
forgotten, defaced by graffiti and the legendary
legion's recognition signs. Time's tide creeps
over sandflats, then suddenly surrounds us,
cutting us off, sweeping us all away, until only
these rocks remain.

The Poet

Guests gathering, like evening shadows, a fuzziness
at the edge of dark and light: "The poet? I knew him
well. He stood there, where you stand now, talking to
me, sharing his word magic." They knew him well,

Knew him better than I did. Or did they? *"From this
corner one could see the interior sea."* If it were not
for the walls that surround this city. Words in a bar
are not words on a page; words exchanged by letter,

By telephone, or by e-mail are not weighted words
inlaid with gems of perspicacity. What are they, then,
these words that shake our world, that move us to act?

I think of the times we met. The poems we exchanged,
and I think of him as I sit and drink at the bar, writing
"so as no to feel alone for centuries of centuries."

'Desde esta cárcel podría verse el mar.'
'... por no sentirme solo, por los siglos de los siglos.'
José Hierro : Reportaje.

After the Reading

Many names were dropped to lie scattered on the floor.
Some of them broke. Others bounced back to their feet.
They walked around stiffly, smiling unhappily.

Sugar and saccharine, unnameable sweetness, all lay
on the ground surrounded by hollow metaphors,
accumulated clichés, vague imagery, empty shells,

blanched bones of half-remembered quotes, once learned by
heart, the full regalia of a master poet's flesh and blood.

After the party, when the cleaner came, she swept
away the remains: dead words, living once upon a time,
now huddled and heaped in a common ossuary,

dust without love, cigarette butts and smoke, nothingness
by definition, emptiness, empty nests, all empathy lacking,
the palest shadows of another man's words and dreams.

Towering Dust

Plaza de las Losillas

Only the bell tower remains. Millennial nests
rest on a bedrock of brick and worked stone.
Granite, the lower rows, and granite the original
hands that toiled, bullying the stone into shape,

making these masonic marks, this cross, that angle,
that snub-nosed C, cherubic in its innocence, letters
written across the years to signify that so-and-so
was here, his name forgotten, his sign carved here

and there, on stones across Europe, a master mason
called to the most catholic enterprise of multiple
churches, built in the savior's name, and now this

tower, dust to dust, all that remains, with its mason's
name, or rather, his sign, carved in these few stones
still climbing skywards, still challenging earth and sky.

Five Poems from *The Empress of Ireland* (2007)

A Survivor Lights a Candle Before the Main Altar at the Sanctuaire Sainte-Anne During the Latin Mass Pointe-au-Père

I am still afraid of fire:
in principio erat verbum / in the beginning was the word.

I am still afraid of the loud voice of the match
scratching its sudden flare,
narrowing my pupils, enlarging the whites of my eyes:
et lux in tenebris lucet / and light shines in darkness.

Booming and blooming, igniting the soul's dark night, a voice of fire:
et Deus erat verbum / and the Word was God.

Flourishing to nourishment, flames whispering on the flood:
omnia per ipsum facta sunt / all things were made by Him.

Wool and water, this sodden safety blanket;
drowned this plush teddy bear, the staring eyes of this doll:
et tenebrae eam non comprehenderunt /
and the darkness comprehended it not.

Their eyelashes bound together with salt,
a silken mist dowsed their drowsing:
hic venit in testimonium / this served as a witness.

Still the patterns pierce my sleep,
hauling me from my opaque dreams,

holding my wrists in this sailor's double clasp:
non erat ille lux / he was not the light.

I hauled my sister up by her hair
only to find her staring eyes
belonging to the already dead:
et mundus eam non cognovit / and the world knew her not.

The moon shone forth upon the waters:
et vidimus gloriam ejus / and we saw His glory.

Crucifix on the Point

Ste. Luce-sur-mer

Eyes open, Christ hangs from the great stone crucifix.
Does he see, out at sea, where gray waves cover
the graveyard of the *Empress*, at rest,
her passengers caressed beneath shallow waters.

They have gone on before me, those friends I numbered,
pierced and piercing their eyes. Last night's footprints fill
with windblown dust and sand; dry crunch of skull
and skeleton crushed underfoot as sea boots ascend the beach.

Unknown, these lands around me:
emitte lucem tuam / send forth Thy light!
Unexplored, these mountains that surround me:
ipsa me deduxerunt / such things have led me on.
Unsolved , these mysteries that confound me:
in montem sanctum tuum / unto Thy holy hill ...
... in nomine Patris / ... in the name of the Father.

Lost Soul

I wander from grave to grave, reading the headstones:
quare me repulisti? / why hast Thou cast me off?

Coarse grass, woven bindweed as columbines combine.
Incessant mourning of glove grey morning doves,
drawing tears from dawn's face:
quare tristis incedo? / why do I go sorrowful?

Verdant stems, unsophisticated flowers,
weeds dark between stark granite stones.
A name, whose name, my long-lost brother's name,
not yet carved in stone, not yet in thy tabernacle:
non in tabernacula tua / not in Thy tabernacle.

The churchyard is as steady as a headland in a storm.
Here, at least, the terrestrial centre is stable:
quare tristis es, anima mea? / why art thou sad, oh my soul?

And the arc on the waters moving from side to side,
lulled by the sea waves, up and down.
On the altar, a gilded chalice, far from the sea's far-flung malice:
quare conturbas me? / why dost thou disquiet me?

A Survivor Contemplates Night Fall

by the Sanctuaire Sainte-Anne
Pointe-au-Père

There is no sanctuary between a rock and a hard place,
no safe haven between this hardness of heart
and the sea rocked chamber where they lie.

Wet weeds bind their feet. Their hands are helpless now.
Death's knot will not of itself willingly untie.

Where now is the sweat from their brow?
What value now the fruit of their labor?
Where lies that rosy-cheeked apple of their eyes?

There is only the lowly hiss of the serpent sea,
the serpentine sea-kiss that sets us all free.

Grey seals, last night, cast concrete shadows
as they slithered up the beach.
If they turned their backs on the sea,
would they turn into one lost child?

The silky cry of their sullen grief ties a knot
in the hollow tube of my throat.

More Survivors Come Ashore

Galérie Marcel Gagnon
Ste. Flavie

What cruel god beached them here, their stone expressions
marooned beneath this concrete sky? Fresh from the sea,
their press gang faces are fixed on this firmament.

They tread watery beds of cockles and muscles.
The waters through which they pass are alive, alive *eaux*.

Being and nothingness: giant panic reaching his hand skywards,
as tall as last night's mushroom-colored clouds.
Looming above the landscape, night's wheelbarrow,
with its womb of dead stars, trundling across the sky.

Up this rock-strewn path the shadows climb, eyes open,
thankful for this touch of land.
Each ill placed step a stumble, and every stumble
a fall from the precipitous face of the lowly cliff.

Knots in the pine rail saw rough beneath their hands.
Iron horse shoe nails pinch heavy with rust.
Splinters drive live wires through water-soft skin
as sodden flesh strips all too easily from the bone.

They have passed through an ordeal of fire:
fire on the flood, fire in the air, fire in the water,
explosions of fire under the water:
the evangelical preaches his biblical hell
and beats his good book blue, like the sea,
and black like these timbers drifting on the water.

Night falls again and again, filling us all with enigmatic stars.

Six Poems from *Obsidian* 22 (2007)

Second Chance

Yesterday, they tied my tongue with thin blades of grass.
Today they sew my lips with threads from dusty spider-webs.
how can there be a tomorrow when sorrow lays
fine layers of sand and silt along the heart's highways?

Now the sun is a marigold, ringed with fire.
Bird song throngs the branches, tiny claws clutch at my heart.
The tree's harp thrives with live-wire melodies.
Cicadas saw their one note harmonies.

Morning strings its seven-seamed rainbow.
Sun threads itself through a needle's eye of cloud.
Wild shadows inhibit the skull's dark cave.

Can worlds be rebuilt with words or must they be constructed
with wild bricks and silence? All my dreams
are gleaned from a stubble of remembered dust.
Midnight stands speckled with mysterious stars.

Sun Block

Last night I got caught between two mirrors.
They stole my soul, flashing it back and forth
between the black holes of their empty spaces.
Now, I am a man of glass, haunted by shadows
that steal my words away, leaving me speechless.

I go to the *brujo* and he seizes me by my wrist,
squeezing it between finger and thumb,
pursuing each heartbeat down its thin, red lane.
He breathes god dust into my eyes and turns me
into an eagle. I soar into the sky on wind-ruffled wings.

I rise to the sun and return with my feathers all aflame.
The exact name for all things is tied to my tongue.
The *brujo* plucks a feather from my breast and I am
a man again. He dips the feather in my blood: Write,"
he says. "Just write." Words of fire descend. They burn
into my flesh, turning old scars into a freshness of flowers.

Doing Yoga on the Azotea

Trapped in this wet, clay rag of a body,
clamped fast in its earthbound snares,
my spirit grinds its teeth as I stretch to face the sun.
Hummingbirds surround me, fanning my face with a whirr of wings.
If I stand still long enough will the world forget that I am here?

"Three thousand larks were sacrificed so the Roi Soleil
might devour one lark tongue pie."

Now no larks rise twittering over vanishing commons.
Vaughan Williams captured their one last song in plastic furrows
where the spirits of those strange incarcerated birds still sing.

I do not want these hummingbirds to become extinct.
I do not want them to become as silent as a skylark, as dead as a dodo,
as *passé* as the carrier pigeons that once thronged our northern woods
and darkened our skies for three whole days.

I once saw a photo of a man.
He stood on top of a sixty-foot pyramid of buffalo skulls.
The snap was shot through a narrow hole in a metal tube with a single
flash of gunpowder from behind a black cloth screen.

"3,500 carrier pigeons were shot in a single afternoon.
1599 buffalo were slaughtered in a day by one man on a horse.
He had 1600 bullets and only one missed the target.
Carcasses littered the plain, like spent and empty shells."
Buffalo survivors now gather in tiny herds.

They no longer shake the earth with their thunder,
but quietly graze in zoos and on buffalo farms.

I want to bend lower and lower until
my head is buried in the *azotea*'s flowers.
I do not want to see the extinction that surrounds me.

Leaves

They have lives of their own, these leaves.
I met one once on the back seat of a bus.
As happy as an elf in autumn, he was going
to see his cousin, still living on the Tule tree.

I met another leaf curled up in a *tortilla*.
The merry fellow stole a sliver of *jalapeño*
and was beamed up on a sunbeam
that descended through the sky's open door.

The trees' verbiage, they are, thick on tongue,
lively in the mind. They conjugate fresh
beginnings to new means, middles, and ends.

Gathering in past participles, they age and lie
thick upon the ground. They also wax lively
on winds that blow cobwebs from the mind.

Lost! Lost! We are all lost and drifting.
Yet still the leaves flood forwards, claiming
to hold the secret that will open our world
and present us with the pearl within the oyster.

Old Man from Arrozola

The skin of his hands is thick and heavy,
the leather pelt of a working animal.
His finger nails are claws. His bare feet
poke out from an old car tire bound
with leather: rough hewn footwear
he has created for himself.

His toe nails are *clavos*, nails of iron,
a climber's spikes gripping the earth.
cut off from the man, they protrude
from a diabolical cloven hoof.
For a moment, horned and tailed,
he dances in a devil suit, black smoke
with red and orange flames.

Now his eyes are as clear as the water
he drinks from my bottle. We sit on
the temple steps at Monte Albán,
in a narrow line of shade that deflects
the sun's obsidian blade.

Each shadow is a fine-lined slash
bisecting the dry dust, dividing
the day into hot and cold.

Don Nadie

At midnight, squads of black shadows take over the *zócalo.*
Nobody asks them for a match.
Nobody invites them to walk down the alley to a cheap hotel.

Dogs sniff the wind. Beggars pretend they are not there.
The *brujo* from Yalalag sees things that others do not see.
"¡*Hermanos*! He smiles. "I too have lost my way."

Who is the one that leaves this place and returns to all places,
all places being one when the hands on the clock
stand to attention, vertical, at midnight, as the owl calls?

No! I am not sane. Nor will I ever be the same again.
Sometimes I think I know who I am, but I don't,
especially when the carnival mask covers my face
or when the razor draws its thin red scratch
cross the dry husks of my soul.

Seven Poems from *Land of Rocks and Saints* (2008)

Juglar / Juggler

1

In the beginning was the word,
and the word was tossed in the air
like a dove over dark water.

It grew as it descended,
turned into tongues of flame,
each of them licking
at the listeners' hearts,
tearing them apart.

Sleight of hand:
this deck of words, tossed skywards;
jacks and queens tumbling,
caught, tossed up again;
words, nothing but words,
this pack of wolves descending.

Juglar / Juggler

2

Lips part as words draw blood;
red wound of the open mouth,
a rose in spring's garden
bears us down with crimson scents.

The spirit flaps trapped in its cage,
flesh and bone binding those wings
with their urgent urge to be free and fly ....

"*... you would have seen ...*" he says.
And so we see: the sea, white horses cresting,
St. James riding over the mountains,
bone on lance point, spear bloodied,
Moorish chain mail bursting asunder,
El Cid advancing on his foes.

Words join with words,
become joint with gesture;
they plunge into our chests,
throw a tight noose
around heart and lungs.

Stork Talk

If this stork could talk would it tell the tale of babies
swaddled in cotton, brought crying from the south
to adorn the cribs of burgers and peasants standing
below the cathedral with its stork perch high above?

Or would it tell the tale of the tile in the tourist shop:
"Don't believe in stupid storks: find love, get pregnant!"
The world is changing and has changed. Storks ranging
over once open fields see a crimson tide of brick raging

against the city's walls. Castille's interior sea, indeed:
but the sea has suffered a sea change, turning from green
and gold to red, banded with broad black tarmac threads

tying down the countryside. Storks now gather at garbage
dumps and their former hunting grounds are stalked by
bulldozers, cement mixers, and long-necked, metal cranes.

Bells

Waves on this interior sea, life moving in and out,
rising and falling to the swell of rhythmic bells,
pounding, breaking their sea-surf over slate grey
roofs, stone walls breaking the water of the bell-

ways, whirlpools in back alleys, trapped in eddies,
rippling round and round, rebounding, hammering
at heart and head. Sudden, this silence, this absence
of bells. This city is built on the bones of the dead:

cobbled spirits cluster, clutch at the heart, crowding
like bells, gripping the heart space between arterial
walls where the city still pumps its blood red surge,

men and women, corpuscles in this heart throb, walk
here there, everywhere, in rhythm to the ... bells have
again begun beneath a pulsing sun their urgent clamor.

Small Corner

And this is the good thing,
to find your one small corner
and to have your one small candle,
then to light it, and to leave it burning
its sharp bright hole in the night.

Around you, the walls you constructed;
inside, the reduced space, the secret garden,
the holy of holies where roses grow
and no cold wind disturbs you.

"Is it here?" you ask: "Or over here?"
If you do not know, I cannot tell you.

But I will say this: turning a corner one day
you will suddenly know that you have found a perfection
that you will seek again, in vain, for the rest of your life.

Secular Saint

She keeps watch over the bar. I beckon.
She leans towards me. Not just her face,
but her care-worn hands, her whole body,
the tender, slender trunk of her, doubled

upon itself, her role cast here in shadows,
in black and white images, stark, twinned
again in the bar's multiple mirrors. She
watches me watching her every movement,

every moment. Again she is here before me,
among the pots and pans, amidst the dishes,
washing, wiping, cleaning, stripping, frying,

moving chairs, turning tables, doing and undoing,
no task too low, too dirty, too menial, too onerous …

« También entre los pucheros de la cocina anda el Señor. »
"The Lord also walks in the kitchen among the pots and pans."
St. Teresa of Avila

Words

They never came from me, these words:
like water in a well, they were just there,
building upwards, like clouds in air,
or ice or snow flakes, crystals gathering.

Words, like heat, bounce from granite walls;
stone squares, cobbled streets where human chessmen strut;
each man a pawn, it seems,
though some grow mighty in their dreams.

Ávila: granite ship, this rock of ages,
sailing its interior sea of gold and green.
Nobody can swim against this ocean of stone.

Poor jack tars, leaping into everyday life,
laboring for this daily bread that dallies
with wine, upon their lips.

Sunset:
the sun's gold medal cooling itself in a silver mist.

Five Poems from *All About Angels* (2009)

The Lost Angel

One day she was there,
the next day she was not.
We never noticed her
slipping through our fingers,
like water or sand.

We glanced away,
and when we looked up,
she had gone.

She had joined the host
of lost children who play
in secret on empty sands.

We wanted to join them,
but when they sensed
our presence, the children
slid swiftly away
and hid in silence
until we had left the beach.

Now the wind whispers their secrets.
The sea grass wags its tongue.
The waves walk word prints
over a silent barren beach.

Boxed Angel

She lies there,
in her wooden box,
so silent.

A Christmas present
or a birthday gift
waiting to be opened.

Her lips are glazed
with a streak of carmine.
Her cheeks are rouged.

What can we do with her now?
We can't take her home.

We turn away.
The sad man puts the lid
back on her box
and returns her
to her refrigerated drawer.

Christmas Angel

When he opens his mouth,
his tongue falls bleeding on the silver tray
passed round to collect the money.

Once upon a time he sang carols
but now he chokes
on red herring bones
and obscure meanings.

His knees are dusty from lack of use.
What wooden doll's head rocks on his shoulders?

On Christmas Eve,
a painted clothes peg lies in the cradle.

He swaddles it with birdsong
and mimes unwritten words
to half-remembered tunes.

Lonely Angel

We found him
hanging from a tree.

His swollen tongue
the clapper of a blue, blue bell
licking in the wind
at a slice of lips.

When we cut him down,
he folded like a pack of cards,
all value peeled away
in fifty-two
faceless moments.

I opened a door in my head
to let in the sunlight.

It filtered through high
leafless branches,
until a broken bell sounded
its cracked chime in my mind.

Black Angel

You cannot hide
when the black angel comes
and knocks on your door.

"Wait a minute!" you say,
"While I change my clothes
and comb my hair."

He shakes his head
and is there before you,
in the clothes closet,
pulling your arm.

You move to the bathroom
to brush your teeth.

"Now!" says the angel.

Your eyes mist over.
You know you are there,
but you can no longer see
your reflection in the mirror.

Other books by Roger Moore,
available online at Amazon and Kindle,
include the following titles.

A Cancer Chronicle
All About Angels
Avila
Bistro
(Finalist, New Brunswick Book of the Year, 2016)
Bistro Two
Empress of Ireland
Iberian Interludes
Monkey Temple
Nobody's Child
Obsidian's Edge
Sun and Moon
Though Lovers Be lost

On Being Welsh
in a land ruled by the English
(available from Cyberwit.net)

You can follow Roger Moore online at

rogermoorepoet.com

https://www.amazon.com/author/rogermoorepoet

www.ingramcontent.com/pod-product-compliance
Lightning Source LLC
Chambersburg PA
CBHW022157160726
48282CB00024B/227
* 9 7 8 8 1 8 2 5 3 7 1 8 7 *